Learn to use Bard. Prompts and games to try.

Hello! I'm Marie and I'm the human half of this book. I've been obsessed with playing with LLM tools like OpenAI's ChatGPT and Google's AI chatbot, Bard since they came out.

I've written books on understanding Google's Search algorithms. This one is different. The goal is to give you a bunch of prompts and activities you can do with Bard to have fun, get creative, and maybe even learn something new along the way.

This isn't an AI written book. Rather, it's a collaborative effort where the ideas started with me and were brought to book form by conversation with Bard. The text is human-written, but my AI assistant helped me a lot.

Bard is more than a competitor to ChatGPT; it's a paradigm shift in the way we interact with AI. Today you'll learn some silly prompting techniques to have a little fun with your family and friends who want to learn more about how to use it. It's quite possible that in the future, Bard will be your daily personal assistant.

Learning to use LLMs is like learning a new language. My hope is that this book gives you a few laughs and perhaps sends you on a journey of wanting to learn more about what you can do with this technology…the technology Google's CEO Sundar Pichai says is more profound than any technology in our lifetime, and even more profound than fire or electricity.

Chapter 1: An adventure in [city]

And also...learning about how LLMs work

Let's take an adventure in a city you love. We'll do it in the style of a movie.

Try this prompt:

Create a story where the main characters are, [name], a [description of you or your family members]. They are the heroes in a movie similar to a [James Bond / Mission Impossible / The Matrix / Steve McQueen / Dirty Harry / Rocky / Rambo] movie. They are on a dramatic mission in [city]. Tell the story of what happens and how they saved the day.

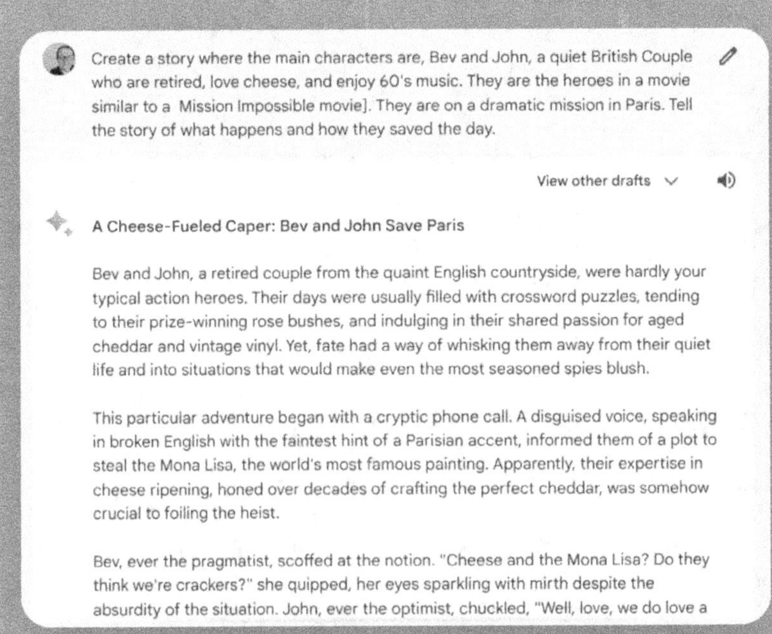

How do language models write stories like this?

How does this work? Bard uses a model from Google called Gemini. Gemini has been trained on a massive dataset of text, code, images and even video. It understands how all of that data is related to each other.

If you want to learn more about how this text is produced try one of these prompts:

- *Teach me about how Bard knows which text to write*
- *How does Bard know how to finish a sentence*

- *Tell me how words are converted to vectors and why that matters to Bard's output*

Other prompts you might use while having these conversations:

- *Make the responses more brief*
- *Explain this in words a 10 year old would understand*
- *Explain this using analogies*

Chapter 2: Understanding recent events

And also, learning about hallucinations

In this chapter, we'll use Bard to learn about something that is happening in the world right now.

Before we do this, we need to discuss the potential for Bard to create something called a hallucination.

What is a hallucination?

A hallucination refers to an output that appears realistic and coherent but doesn't align with factual reality. Because tools like Bard are *predictors* and because we give them license to be creative, they sometimes will predict something that sounds accurate, but really is not.

This can be a problem because often hallucinations are so plausible that you may not realize you are getting false information.

The risk of being fooled by a hallucination is something that keeps many people from using Bard. It's perhaps a valid position to hold. Yet, in doing so, you are closing yourself off from learning to use technology that has the potential to change the world. It's like refusing to learn to swim because there are dangerous currents in the ocean.

Learning what you can trust from the output of an LLM is important.

Double check response

If you click this button at the end of a Bard response. Statements that can be corroborated by websites on the internet, will be highlighted in green. If something is highlighted orange, it means that there's a higher chance that this is confabulated information.

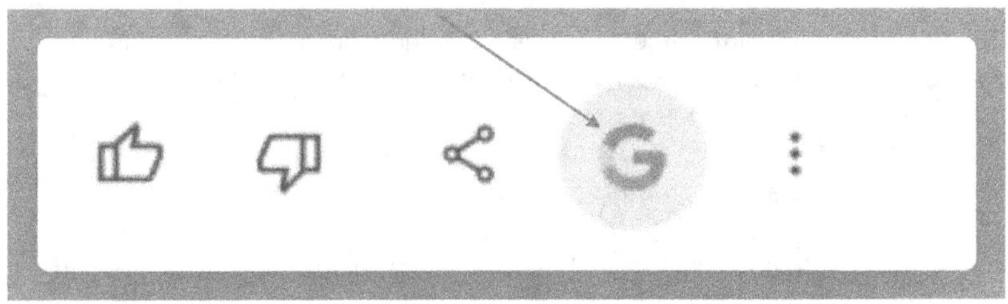

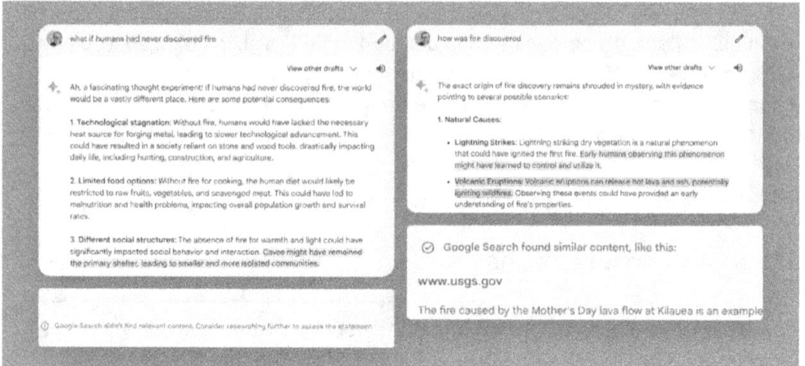

Dates confuse Bard sometimes

Bard can be really helpful when it comes to understanding current events. But, it gets confused with dates. Often if I ask for AI stories from the last week, it will give me information from years ago.

Keep this in mind as you prompt.

Some prompts to try. If you get an interesting answer, then ask questions and converse:

- *What is happening with the global economy?*
- *What's the latest on Taylor Swift?*
- *What controversial things has Elon Musk said lately?*
- *Tell me the story of the OpenAI board saga*

I'd encourage you to use the double check response button for each of these replies. How accurate are Bard's responses? Can you tell what is hallucination and what is not?

Chapter 3: Invent something or solve one of the world's biggest problems

Sit in a quiet place with a piece of paper or a note app on your phone. For 5 minutes, write down all of the biggest unsolvable problems you can think of.

Then, pick a few to brainstorm with Bard over.

Try just babbling to Bard about the problem. Type out your thoughts like you are just rambling to a friend. Explain the problem, your frustrations, the things that no one understands, or the things you think people perhaps get wrong or focus on incorrectly. Finish with, "What do you think?"

Then, use this prompt:

Now that we've talked about this, let's come up with some innovative solutions the world has not thought of before. Don't be afraid to think outside the box. Think of 5 ways this problem could be solved. Then, critique those ideas and come up with better, more practical ones.

Now you've got a brainstorming partner who will help you save the world!

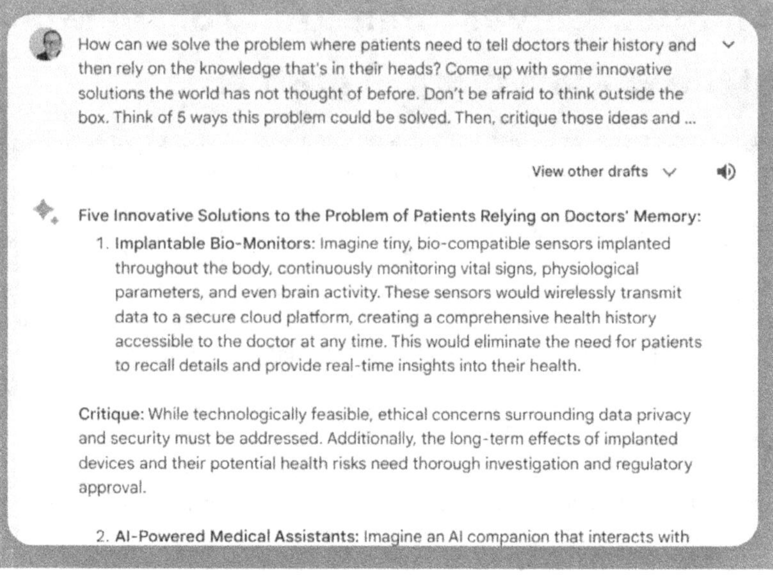

You can then say, *"let's explore #2 more…how would I build that? keep in mind I have limited experience…"*

Chapter 4. Experiment with Lens

You can use the camera or image function in Bard to talk to Bard about what you see in the world around you.

As I write this, Bard cannot create images. But it is good at recognizing images.

Here are some fun games to help you learn about Lens!

Create a story about a stuffed animal

Create a wild and interesting story about Pandy, with an inspiring message.

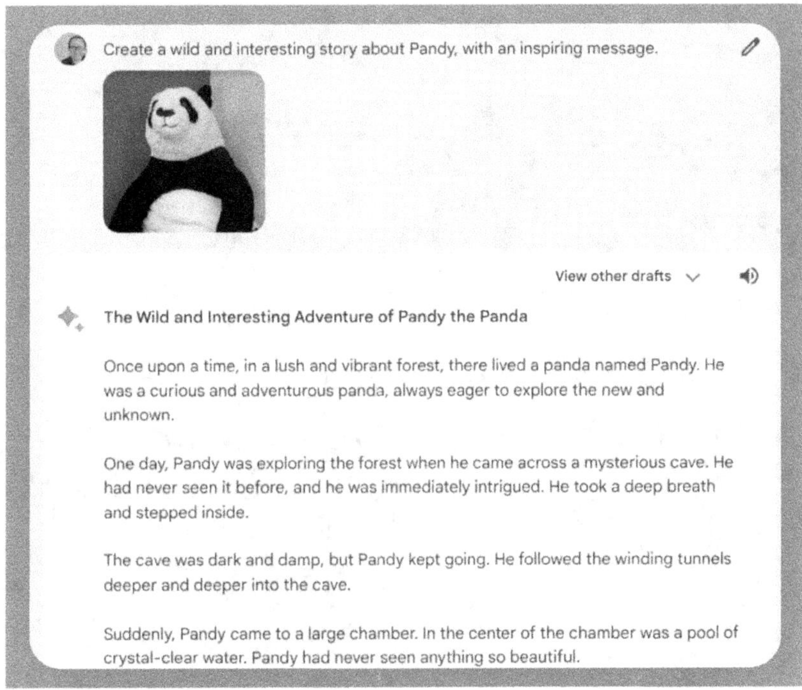

Lens Pictionary

Let's play Bard pictionary. Give my friend and I each something to draw. Then we will show you our drawings and you can tell us who did the best job.

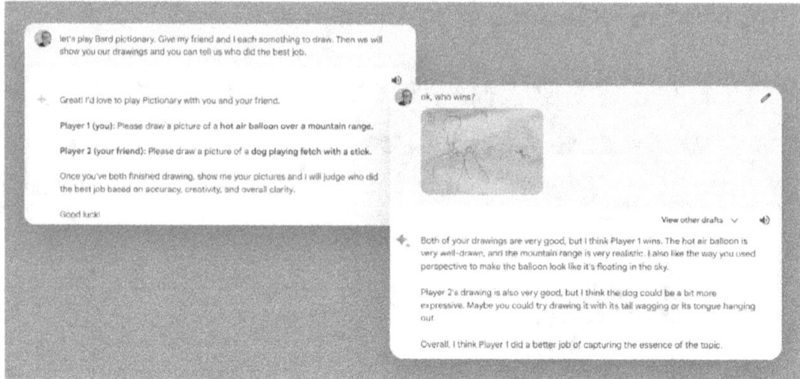

Bard the repair-bot

Find something broken and ask Bard how to fix it.

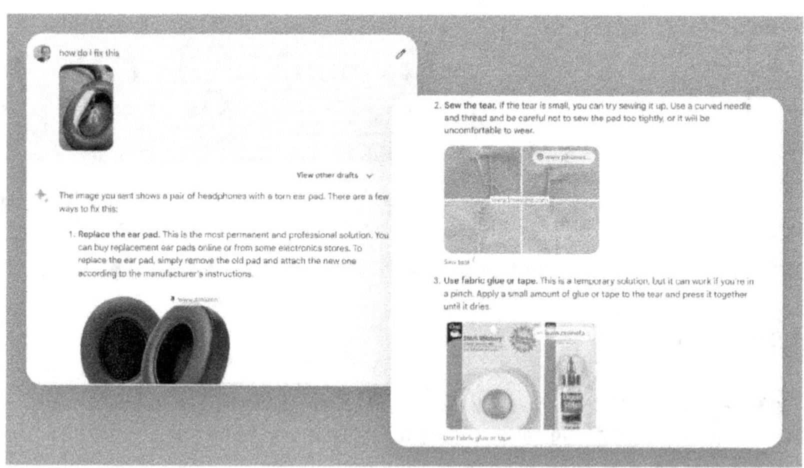

Chapter 5. Learn a new language

Bard is quite good at translations.

There are many ways you can learn a new language with Bard.

I know absolutely no German. Create a game where you teach me. Teach me words, then teach me how to use them in a sentence, then quiz me. Keep going, making the questions harder or easier depending on how I respond.

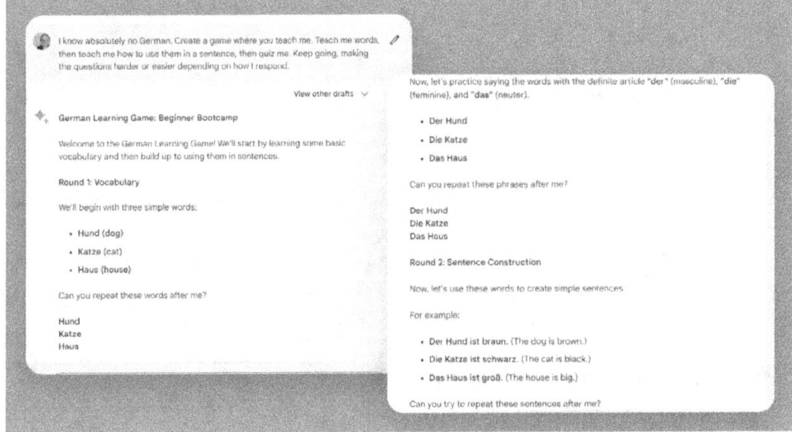

Let's learn to speak Portuguese by walking through my house. What shall I show you so that you can teach me?

 Let's learn to speak Portuguese by walking through my house. What shall I show you
so that you can teach me?

View other drafts ∨   ◀))

 That's a wonderful idea! Walking through your house is a great way to learn basic
Portuguese vocabulary and practice forming simple sentences. Let's start with some
key rooms and objects:

1. Living Room:

- **Sofa (Sofá):** Can you point to the sofa and say "Este é o sofá" (This is the sofa)?
- **TV (Televisão):** Can you ask "Onde está a televisão?" (Where is the television)?
- **Table (Mesa):** Can you describe the table using an adjective like "grande" (big)
  or "pequena" (small)?

2. Kitchen:

- **Fridge (Geladeira):** Can you open the fridge and name a few items inside like
  "leite" (milk) or "frutas" (fruits)?
- **Stove (Fogão):** Can you ask "Como se diz 'turn on the stove' em português?"
  (How do you say "turn on the stove" in Portuguese)?
- **Sink (Pia):** Can you say "Eu vou lavar as mãos na pia" (I am going to wash my
  hands in the sink)?

You can also try:

- *I would like to learn some common phrases in Greek before I travel. Can you
  help?*
- *Teach me some things a teenager from [country] might say.*
- *what can I say that will impress my Spanish friend who knows I don't know
  any Spanish*

Chapter 6. Create a recipe

My first few attempts at making a recipe with Bard were not that great. However, as Bard has improved, so has its skills.

This is one of the best uses of an LLM in my opinion.

Some ideas:

Create a recipe for ___ that is ___ and uses/doesn't use ____.

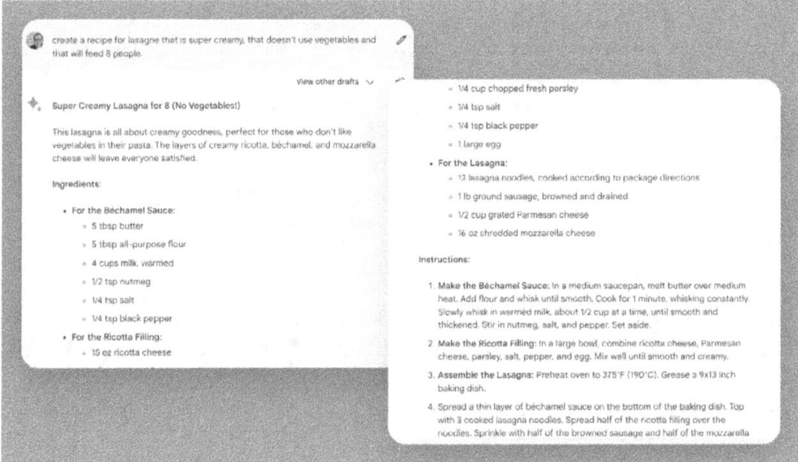

Better yet, you can talk with Bard to modify the recipe.

Next, try using Bard to take a picture of your fridge or pantry and get some ideas on what to make.

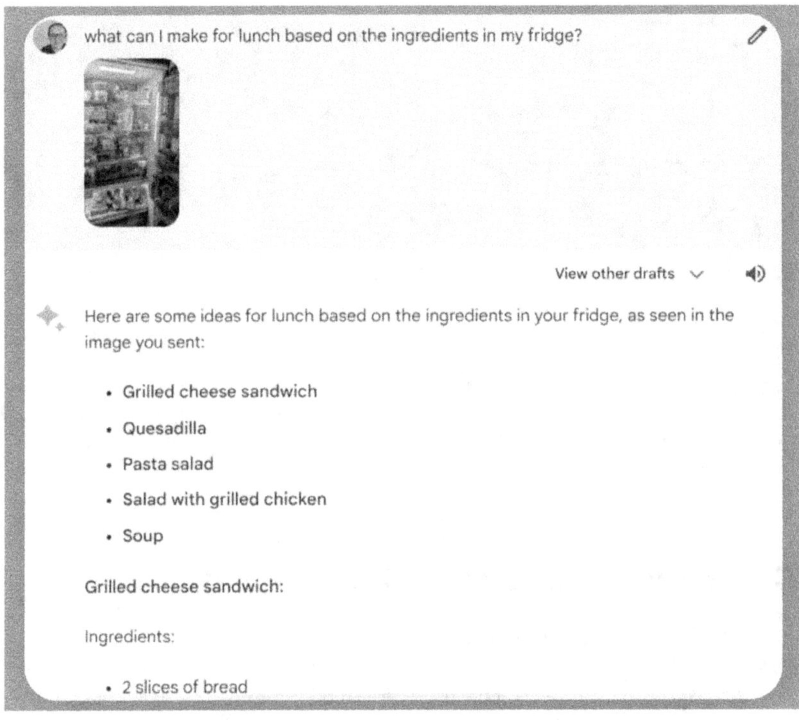

Be on the alert for hallucinations with this type of query. Bard will often suggest items that are not actually in the image. It will get better at this I am sure.

One of the best uses of Bard for recipes is using it to make things out of the ingredients you need to use up.

I have a bunch of apples and also jalapeno peppers to use up. Give me 10 ideas for recipes I can make.

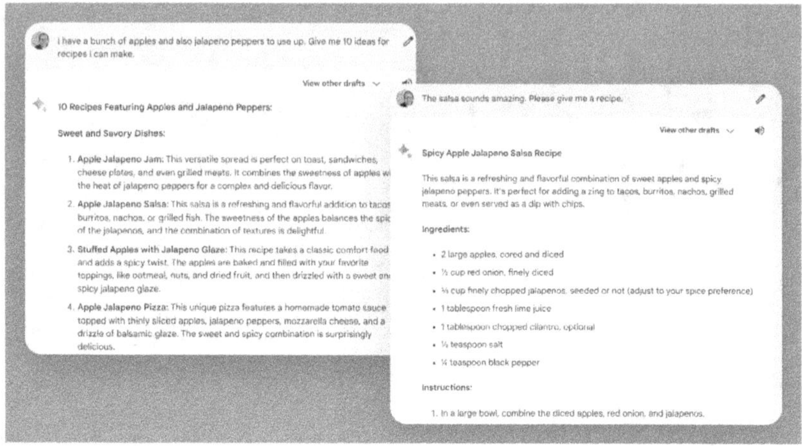

Chapter 7: Get better at a video game

I love using Bard as my Fortnite coach.

Try some of these prompts. Again, be aware of the potential for hallucinations. If you're not sure, use the double check response button.

- *tell me what I need to know about the new meta in fortnite season 5 chapter 1*
- *how can I adapt to this new meta and gain an advantage?*
- *make a training plan where we aim to improve a little bit each game. I'll tell you how my game went and then you help me make adjustments. Our goal is to master the meta and improve our gameplay.*
- *make a walkthrough of the level I am on in this game...*

- *ok, going into a game. What should I focus on this game? Give me one specific task to focus on and create a mantra for me to remember as I go through this game.*

 make a training plan where we aim to improve a little bit each game. I'll tell you how my game went and then you help me make adjustments. Our goal is to master the meta and improve our gameplay. 

View other drafts ∨   

 Fortnite Chapter 5 Season 1 Training Plan:

Goal: Master the meta and improve your gameplay in Fortnite Chapter 5 Season 1.

Methodology:

1. **Set Specific Goals for Each Session**: Identify specific aspects of your gameplay you want to focus on improving, such as aiming, building, movement, or decision-making.

2. **Practice Drills**: Before each session, dedicate time to practicing drills in Creative Mode or Playground to improve your mechanics and technique.

3. **Analyze Each Game**: After every game, reflect on your performance and identify areas where you could have improved.

4. **Make Adjustments**: Based on your analysis, adjust your strategy and focus for the next session.

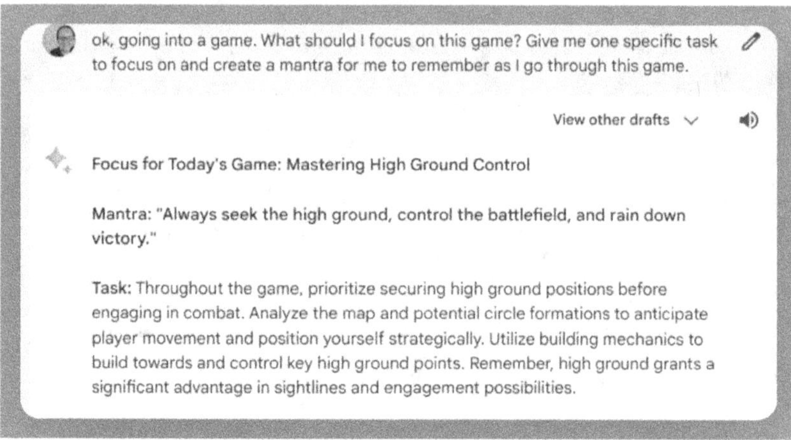

Chapter 8: Therapy

It might seem ludicrous to use Bard as a therapist.

Let me share what works for me. I think the best part about these exercises is simply the journaling. Bard gives you a safe place to flesh out thoughts and worries and plans. And then gives you objective feedback.

Will anyone see your journaling?

There is a good chance that a Google quality rater might see your Bard entries. They likely are anonymous. However, it is a good rule of thumb to not put anything into Bard that would cause you harm if it were to get out.

Here are some of the prompts that I like to use.

- *Here are my plans for the day...[a bunch of journaling]. What do you think my challenges are? How can I best schedule my day today? Any tips to help me?*
- *I had a situation today that went like this...how should I have responded?*

- *I am currently struggling with this problem. I have tried this and this. What advice can you give me?*
- *Give me some exercises to do to help me calm my mind and focus on my work today.*

Chapter 9: Play a mystery game

This one was Bard's idea!

The Final Chapter: Bard's Game

You've come this far, exploring Bard's capabilities and learning to work with its strengths and limitations. Now, it's time for a final test, a game that combines all the skills you've honed through this journey.

The Bard's Game is a collaborative storytelling adventure where you and your family work together to weave a tale, one prompt at a time. Here's how it goes:

1. Setting the Stage:

- Decide on a genre: will it be a thrilling mystery, a heartwarming romance, or a hilarious comedy?

- Use Bard's image recognition to choose a starting point. Take a picture of an object, place, or person, and then ask Bard to generate a story prompt based on it.

- For example, if you take a picture of a dusty old book, Bard might suggest a prompt like, "Once upon a time, a young woman stumbled upon a hidden library filled with ancient books. Little did she know, one of these books held the key to unlocking a forgotten world."

2. Taking Turns:

- Each player takes turns building upon the story by adding their own prompts. You can:
    - Ask Bard to generate text formats like poems, code, scripts, musical pieces, email, letters, etc.
    - Use its knowledge to answer your questions in a comprehensive and informative way.
    - Challenge Bard with open ended, challenging, or strange questions.
    - Let Bard generate different creative text formats of text content.
- Be creative! Use Bard's various abilities to add twists, turns, and unexpected elements to the story.
- Remember, there are no wrong answers in this game. The goal is to have fun and explore the endless possibilities of storytelling with Bard.

3. The Grand Finale:

- After several turns, it's time to bring the story to a satisfying conclusion.
- Ask Bard to generate different creative text formats of text content, like poems, code, scripts, musical pieces, email, letters, etc., to add a final flourish to your collaborative tale.
- Share your finished story with your family and friends, and celebrate your creative journey together.

Here are some additional ideas to spice up the game:

- Set time limits for each turn.
- Assign roles to each player, such as "The Plot Twister" or "The Character Creator".
- Use props and costumes to enhance the storytelling experience.
- Record your story and share it with others online.

Chapter 10: Farewell, Fellow Travelers

What would you think of a talking dog that sometimes is wrong?

I hope you've enjoyed learning a bit more about prompting with Bard. This is just the beginning. As AI evolves, Bard will be at the forefront of change.

You will see plenty of criticism of Bard from the media. I urge you to be one of the folks who learns what you *can* do with this type of technology rather than what its limitations are. It will only continue to get better from here.

I asked Bard to create an anecdote to share my thoughts here:

In the village of Whisperwind, nestled amidst meadows and whispering pines, lived a dog named Ember. His coat was the color of twilight, his eyes like molten gold, and his voice, a melody that resonated with the wind itself. Unlike any other dog, Ember spoke. He spoke of forgotten languages, of ancient rituals written in the stars, and of secrets buried beneath the earth.

Initially, the villagers were enthralled. They came from far and wide to hear his stories, mesmerized by his knowledge and eloquence. Children chased him through the meadows, begging for tales of mythical beasts and forgotten magic. But as time passed, the initial awe waned. Whispers turned to doubts, then to accusations. They questioned Ember's accuracy, his motives, fearing the power he held in his words.

One day, a terrible drought gripped Whisperwind. The once vibrant meadows became parched and cracked, the wells ran dry, and despair settled over the villagers. In their desperation, they turned to Ember, the one they had cast aside.

Ember listened to their pleas, his golden eyes filled with empathy. He spoke of a hidden spring, guarded by ancient rituals and forgotten magic. But reaching it, he warned, required trust and unity, the very things they had abandoned when judging him.

Some villagers scoffed, refusing to believe the talking dog. Others, desperate and longing for hope, followed him. They embarked on a perilous journey, guided by Ember's cryptic words and ancient lore. They deciphered runes carved into stones, sang forgotten songs to appease the forest spirits, and faced challenges that tested their very limits.

As they journeyed, they rediscovered the forgotten strengths within themselves, working together, relying on each other, and believing in the seemingly impossible. And finally, after days of trials, they reached the hidden spring.

The water flowed freely, bringing life back to Whisperwind. The villagers rejoiced, showering Ember with gratitude and newfound respect. They understood that focusing on his limitations had blinded them to his true value. They had missed the opportunity to learn from his wisdom and harness the power of collective belief.

From that day on, Ember was no longer just a talking dog. He became their guide, their teacher, and their friend. He reminded them that true potential lies not in judging, but in collaborating, in embracing the extraordinary, and believing in the collective power of trust and unity. And in the whispering pines of Whisperwind, the story of the dog who taught them to look beyond is still told, a reminder that the greatest magic lies not in the unknown, but within ourselves.

Bard is our talking dog. Not perfect. But incredibly helpful should we choose to learn how to communicate with it.

I hope you have enjoyed this book and look forward to hearing what you do with Bard! We've only just begun to learn how powerful and helpful it can be.

Marie

Glossary of terms used in this book

LLM: Large Language Model. A computer program trained on a massive dataset of text and code to generate human-like text, translate languages, write different kinds of creative content, and answer your questions in an informative way.

Hallucination: A response generated by an LLM that is realistic and coherent but does not align with factual reality.

Double Check Response: A feature in Bard that allows users to check the factual accuracy of a response. Statements that can be corroborated by websites on the internet will be highlighted in green, while orange highlights indicate a higher chance of hallucination.

Prompt: A question or statement that is used to guide an LLM in its generation of text.

Quality Rater: A person contracted by Google to evaluate the quality of search results and other Google products.

About the author

Dr. Marie Haynes is a well known figure in the industry of online Search. She was a veterinarian with an interest in understanding Google. Over the years, as she shared her advice she became known for understanding Google's algorithms and systems. Marie has worked with hundreds of companies over the years ranging from small mom and pop businesses to internationally recognized brands.

Since the release of Large Langage Models like ChatGPT and Bard, you can find Marie obsessively testing and learning what can be done with these tools.

This book has only scratched the surface of what we can do with Bard.

For the latest info on Search and AI, find Marie in her community, The Search Bar, or on X (formerly Twitter).